BLUEBIRD RESCUE

A HARROWSMITH COUNTRY LIFE NATURE GUIDE

JOAN RATTNER HEILMAN

CAMDEN
•HOUSE•

PUBLISHING

Camden House Publishing, Inc.

A division of Telemedia Communications (USA) Inc.

Library of Congress Cataloging-in-Publication Data
Heilman, Joan Rattner.
    Bluebird rescue / by Joan Rattner Heilman.
        p.   cm. – (A Harrowsmith country life nature guide)
    Reprint. Originally published: New York : Lothrop, Lee & Shepard Books, © 1982.
    Includes index.
    Summary: Explains the nesting, feeding, and breeding habits of bluebirds and instructs how to protect this endangered species.
        ISBN 0-944475-24-8 (softcover).
        ISBN 0-944475-27-2 (lib. bdg.).
    1. Bluebirds – Juvenile literature. 2. Birds, Protection of – Juvenile literature. 3. Birds, Attracting of – Juvenile literature. [1. Bluebirds. 2. Birds – Protection. 3. Birds – Attracting. 4. Wildlife conservation.] I. Title. II. Series.
QL696.P288H44   1992   91-40618
639.9′78842 – dc20   CIP
                                                                        AC

Design by Eugenie S. Delaney
Front and back cover photographs by Michael L. Smith

Trade distribution by
Firefly Books
250 Sparks Avenue
Willowdale, Ontario
Canada M2H 2S4

Printed and bound in Canada by
D.W. Friesen & Sons Ltd., Altona, Manitoba

CONTENTS

This Eastern female is kept very busy feeding her hungry brood from sunrise to sunset.

WHERE HAVE ALL THE BLUEBIRDS GONE?

If you have ever seen a bluebird, you are really lucky. Most people haven't, even though not very many years ago these shy little thrushes flashed around almost everybody's backyard. When your grandparents were young, bluebirds were almost as common as robins are today. From the time of the first settlers, they have been America's favorite bird.

With their radiant blue feathers, soft round bodies, appealing little faces, and gentle manner, bluebirds came to symbolize hope, happiness, springtime, and love.

More songs were written about them than about any other bird in our history, and one famous writer, Henry David Thoreau, said that bluebirds carry the sky on their backs.

In some parts of North America, which is the only place in the world where bluebirds are found (except Bermuda), you can still find them raising broods of babies in the spring and summer. Perhaps you've even seen a few dozen of them flying south on sunny days in the fall, once known as "bluebird weather."

But the bluebird population has been

The differences among the species can be seen in the Mountain Bluebird (*top*), the Western Bluebird (*bottom*), and the Eastern Bluebird (*page 7*).

shrinking and, a few years ago, these beautiful native birds were in serious danger of becoming extinct, vanishing from the earth forever, just as many other birds and animals already have. Only recently, with the help of people like you, have they begun to thrive again. All over the land, more and more bluebirds can be seen flying through the skies, brightening our lives.

There are three species of bluebirds. Those that have been in the greatest danger are the Eastern Bluebirds (scientific name: *Sialia sialis*), the little blue-backed, rosy-breasted birds that you see so often on greeting cards. Scientists estimate that there is now only one Eastern Bluebird for every ten that lived only forty years ago. The numbers of Mountain (*Sialia currucoides*) and Western (*Sialia mexicana*) Bluebirds, the other two species, had been growing smaller, too, though not as quickly.

The bluebirds' biggest problem is a serious housing shortage. Their habitat is disappearing under layers of concrete and asphalt. Houses, highways, shopping centers, parking lots, industries, huge commercial farms, and railroads have taken over much of the land that once was home to bluebirds and to many other native birds like woodpeckers, nuthatches, and great

This pair of Eastern Bluebirds makes it easy to see why bluebirds were once called "blue robins."

blue herons.

In addition, bluebirds are extremely fussy about where they make their nests. They won't nest in cities or crowded suburbs and they dislike forests or deep shade. Instead, they insist on open spaces, with not too many trees or buildings around them. They will nest only in small enclosures or holes, and they have always loved rotten wooden fence posts, dark hollows in decaying trees, knotholes, and abandoned woodpecker holes. Unfortunately, today most fences are made of metal, dead tree limbs are often zapped by chain saws, and there aren't as many open fields and meadows around as there were even twenty years ago.

Of course, not every natural nesting hole is gone, but those that remain are usually taken over by a couple of other birds — immigrants from Europe. These two tough birds, starlings and house sparrows (formerly called English sparrows), were imported from England during the last century and, because they found few natural enemies here, they soon became the most common birds in many parts of the continent. House sparrows arrived in America by invitation from well-meaning bird lovers in the 1850s. Starlings came in 1880 when eighty of them were released in New York's Central Park. They loved it there. They loved it everywhere they went.

Unfortunately for bluebirds, starlings and house sparrows also like to build their nests in holes, although they will settle for other places. They are much more aggressive than the gentle bluebirds and when there is competition for a hole, they almost always win. If bluebirds or other native birds move into a hole first, starlings and house sparrows often break their eggs or kill the babies, and sometimes even the adult birds as well. Then they may take over the nesting holes.

When starlings and house sparrows move into the holes of hardy, cavity-nesting birds like woodpeckers and chickadees, those birds will flee into the woods to find another place to nest. But bluebirds are not so adaptable. They must have fairly open spaces or they won't nest at all.

Food is another problem. Bluebirds are ground feeders and live mostly on insects. Chemical pesticides used to kill crop-damaging insects may be good for some crops, but they are not good for birds. They kill the insects bluebirds need for food and they may even kill some birds as well.

In late summer and fall and in early spring and winter, bluebirds also eat berries. Starlings are very fond of berries, too,

Starlings, major enemies of bluebirds, compete for nesting holes and almost always win.

House sparrows are another enemy, often breaking bluebird eggs or killing the babies.

and turn out in huge flocks to feast on them. Most of the time, they strip the trees and bushes almost bare so there is very little left for less aggressive birds to eat.

For a while after they came to this continent, starlings and house sparrows made life very difficult only for Eastern Bluebirds. But now those two European birds have gone west, affecting the populations of Mountain and Western Bluebirds as well.

Not all the bluebirds' troubles come from other birds and people. They have natural enemies, too, including bitter cold weather. During some winters, the normally warm areas of North America have been struck by severe cold spells. Each time, many bluebirds have died, from either freezing or starvation, especially when their supply of berries – their main winter food – has been covered with snow and ice. And, of course, bluebirds have to watch out for cats, raccoons, squirrels, and snakes, as well as other predators, including dangerous two-footed human animals, who frequently vandalize their

At the first hint of spring, the male bluebird starts looking for the perfect place for a nest.

nests. All in all, life has become extremely difficult for these little birds.

There is very little that concerned citizens can do to save many of our birds and animals from extinction, except to contribute money to wildlife organizations or to urge their representatives in Congress to pass laws that protect them. But bluebirds are different. Their future depends on the efforts of individuals like you. Their survival is in your hands.

What can you do? You can build bluebird houses, put them up in the right places, and watch over them during the nesting season. When bluebirds move in, you can protect them from their enemies. You can plant bushes or trees or vines with the kinds of berries bluebirds like to eat. And you can ask others to stop using pesticides that kill the birds and the insects they eat. If you think these seem like small steps, you're wrong. For bluebirds to increase in number, they *must* have proper housing and living conditions—it's the only way they can continue to survive.

The North American Bluebird Society was started in 1978 to encourage people to put up bluebird houses, gather information about the birds, and research even better ways to protect them. Its efforts to get people involved in help-

Bluebirds that nest in northern parts of North America must migrate before it gets too cold.

ing these beautiful birds have been so successful that bluebirds are thriving once again, often nesting in areas where they had not been seen for years. But they still need our help.

Dr. Lawrence Zeleny, founder of the society, says, "Bluebirds are well on their way to complete dependence on our help if they are going to survive. With enough effort from us, they can make it. It's entirely up to *us* whether America's favorite bird will live or become only a memory like the passenger pigeon."

WATCHING BLUEBIRDS GROW

Bluebirds belong to the thrush family, which also includes robins and veeries. All thrushes are good singers, eat insects and fruit, and have young with spotted breasts.

The Eastern Bluebird measures about 5½ inches in length—only a little larger than a house sparrow. It has a carpet of rich blue feathers on its head, back, and tail, earthy red feathers on its round breast, and a soft white belly. This species is found from the Atlantic Coast west to the Rocky Mountains, from southern Canada to the Gulf of Mexico, and to the mountains of central Mexico.

The Western Bluebird looks very much like the Eastern Bluebird, but it has a blue throat and the red on its breast extends across its shoulders. It makes its home along the West Coast, from Canada into Mexico.

The Mountain Bluebird breeds in the West, from the western states up through Canada and parts of Alaska, and across the Rocky Mountains, living mainly in meadows and clearings in high altitudes below the timberline. This species is slimmer and slightly longer than the other

A Western male keeps an eye out for his next meal. Notice his blue throat and red shoulders.

they look like adult birds.

Bluebirds are shy birds who rarely raise their voices and usually fight only when they are defending their nests, often losing the battle. They don't sing very loudly and they will never win any awards for their tunes, though many people find nothing more pleasing than their soft, gentle warbling. Someone once said they were saying, "Dear, dear! Think of it, think of it!"

The Mountain and Western species do most of their warbling so early in the morning that they aren't heard very often by human ears. Eastern Bluebirds sound off more frequently as they sit on a

two – about 6 inches from beak to tail – and has no red feathers. It is all bright turquoise blue except for its pale blue belly.

Like many other birds, female bluebirds are much less colorful than the males. Often they look more gray or brown than blue except for the ends of their wings and tails. Young birds, both male and female, are mottled gray with telltale blue around the edges of their wings and tails. Their breasts are speckled, and they look similar to immature robins. In the fall, they molt their baby feathers and by the winter

Mountain Bluebirds are a little larger than the other two species and are bright blue all over.

Two Eastern fledglings, just learning how to fly, sit on a post, gathering the courage to take off.

branch or a fence, hunched over in their round-shouldered way. All bluebirds do their best singing during the short courting season in early spring, when they really go overboard with enthusiasm.

At the first hint of spring, the male bluebird gets busy. He starts hunting for the right hole for a nest. When he finds one, he invites his mate to take a look at it. She is the one who will decide if it is suitable for raising a brood. While she sits on a nearby branch or wire, her fine-feathered mate flies in and out of the hole he has selected and sings just as loudly and beautifully as he can. He flutters his bright blue wings and spreads his blue tail, and brings the female an insect or two to show what a good father he will be. When she finally agrees to enter the hole for an inspection, he encourages her with even more songs.

The female bluebird makes the nest, building the home out of soft dry grasses or fragrant pine needles. Then she lays a clutch of small sky-blue eggs, though once in a while her eggs are pure white. She lays three or four, or even seven or eight, and sits on them to incubate them until they hatch about two weeks later. Meanwhile, the male's job is to guard their home, keep on singing, and bring her a delicious grasshopper or caterpillar now and then. If an

Bluebirds lay small blue eggs in nests made of dry grasses or pine needles and incubate them until they hatch. Below, mother and nestlings.

The father bluebird helps to feed the babies. This time, he brings a tasty young grasshopper.

enemy comes near, the father will chatter and swoop, and sometimes even attack quite fiercely.

Bluebirds also insist upon their territorial rights. This means that they stake out a certain area for themselves and will not allow another bluebird family to live too close by, though other kinds of birds don't bother them as much. Often they will live happily right next door to tree swallows or chickadees or other native birds.

Baby bluebirds, like all little birds, are always very hungry, keeping both parents occupied with bringing them food. Each one of them is fed a tasty insect or a ripe berry about every twenty minutes from before sunrise until after sunset. If there are five or six nestlings, you can see why their mother and father don't have much time for anything else. Meanwhile, the mother also broods the babies, sitting over them to keep them warm until they grow enough feathers to insulate them against the cold.

When the babies are ready to fledge or leave the nest in seventeen to twenty-three days, depending on the species, their parents let them get a little hungry. Then they lure them out of the nest by dangling an insect just out of reach and warbling an encouraging song. Baby bluebirds know instinctively how to fly. They flap their small wings and usually manage to flutter to a nearby tree or bush. For a few weeks, until they learn how to capture their own food, the fledglings are fed and protected by their parents.

Bluebirds often raise two and sometimes three broods of babies every year, so the nesting season may last from February until early September. This keeps everybody busy. The father keeps his eye on the first brood of birds after they leave the nest, making sure they get enough to eat and aren't consumed by cats or raccoons. The mother, meanwhile, gets right to work building a new nest. When a new batch of nestlings is hatched, their older brothers and sisters sometimes help bring them food and the whole family usually stays together in the same neighborhood for the summer.

Bluebirds have a huge appetite for insects, especially those that farmers and gardeners are glad to get rid of, such as cutworms, grasshoppers, crickets, and beetles. They usually catch them by sitting on the limb of a tree, a power line, or a fence post, and then dropping suddenly down to the ground to pounce on their next meal. Mountain Bluebirds like to hover low over the ground in their search for food. When the weather turns cold and insects are scarce, all three species feed mainly on berries.

In warm climates, bluebirds may stay in the same neighborhood all year long. But those that nest in Canada and the northern parts of the United States must migrate before the weather gets too cold. Though years ago bluebirds migrated in

Baby bluebirds know instinctively how to fly. They flap their wings and flutter to a tree.

large flocks, today only about fifteen or twenty of them usually make the trip together. These few families will gradually keep moving south in the fall as the temperatures drop. They will return once again to their old habitats in the early spring.

Male bluebirds spend their time singing, bringing food to the babies, and watching out for enemies.

BUILDING AND MOUNTING NESTING BOXES

If you would like to have bluebird families as your neighbors, then you must provide homes for them. Bluebird nesting boxes must be made to certain specifications so that bluebirds like them and starlings can't fit into them, and mounted where house sparrows won't be too tempted to move in.

The size of the entrance hole is especially important. For Eastern and Western Bluebirds, it must be precisely 1½ inches in diameter – no bigger *or* smaller. If you make it smaller, bluebirds may be unable to get into the house. If you make it even ⅛ inch bigger, starlings may squeeze through.

To accommodate their larger size, Mountain Bluebirds usually do better with an entrance hole that is 1⁹⁄₁₆ inches in diameter. But be careful. If the hole is larger than that, it allows starlings to get in and that's disastrous for bluebirds.

Don't add a perch on the front of the box. Bluebirds don't need one and it gives enemy birds a handy foothold for attacking.

Depth is another important factor. Allow at least 6 inches from the bottom of the entrance hole to the floor so that starlings, cats, raccoons, and other predators will find it difficult to reach the bluebird eggs or baby birds inside.

As for the interior space, most bluebirds do very well in boxes with floor dimensions of 4 by 4 inches. However, if you are making a box for Mountain Bluebirds, increase this to 5 by 5 inches. Mountain Bluebirds are not only a little bigger than Eastern and Western Bluebirds but also tend to lay a larger number of eggs.

To keep the box from becoming too hot or too cold, your birdhouse should be constructed from wood *at least* ¾ inch thick for good insulation. Be sure to cut the corners off the bottom boards to make openings for ventilation and drainage. Good insulation and ventilation are especially important if you live in a very hot climate.

Finally, the nesting box should be easy for you to open for cleaning and observing. But it shouldn't be so easy to open that other people will be tempted to disturb your tenants.

It's simple to make a nesting box if you follow the plans given in the next chapters and are used to handling tools. You can also purchase ready-made nesting boxes from the North American Bluebird Society. The address is P.O. Box 6295, Silver Spring, MD 20916-6295.

For making your own, you can use almost any kind of wood, though most people use western red cedar because it is inexpensive and doesn't need painting. Maybe you can find some old pieces of wood in your basement or garage, enough to make a birdhouse or two. Or you can use *exterior* grade plywood unless there are lots of porcupines in your neighborhood — porcupines like to eat plywood. Do not use pressure-treated lumber because it contains chemicals that may be toxic to birds.

Boxes made of cedar, cypress, or exterior grade plywood need not be painted to make them more durable; however, pine boxes do last longer when painted. If you decide to paint, be sure to choose a *light* color, because it will reflect heat and keep the box cooler than a dark color will. Use exterior latex paint. Or you may finish the outside with natural alkyd wood sealer, spar varnish, or linseed oil. But *do not* paint, seal, stain, or varnish the inside of the box or the edges of the entrance hole and *do not* use chemical wood preservatives.

After you have made your nesting box, you should mount it in the right location, at a certain height, and in a special way if you want to attract bluebirds and watch

Bluebirds have lots of enemies, like this curious flying squirrel, who is investigating a birdhouse.

them raise their families. This is extremely important, even more important than the way you build the house, because bluebirds won't settle in unless the house is located in a place they like.

Bluebirds insist on open land for their housing, with no tall grass or weeds. They prefer cut meadows, grazed fields, and mowed lawns. They like sunshine and space, preferably on a high ridge, with a few scattered trees or high shrubs and fences not more than about 100 feet away in direct view of their front door. This is because fledglings need a safe place to land when they leave the nest for the first time. And adult birds like a high perch so they can spot insects on the ground.

If there aren't enough good natural perches around, you can provide some yourself. Pound some tall stakes or strong tree branches into the ground within 25 feet or so of the box. Also, keep the nearby trees pruned to 9 or 10 feet above the ground and don't cut off the dead limbs because they make excellent perches.

If you don't live on a farm or out in the country, you may need permission to use somebody else's land for your bluebird house. Remember, it should be mounted close enough to your own home so it can be easily monitored during nesting season. Good sites include golf courses, public parks, large cemeteries, college campuses, nature preserves, fields, big lawns and estates, orchards, farmland, meadows, or the edges of rural roads – all open spaces where chemical poisons are not used.

Moving day for bluebirds comes in the early spring. In southern areas, house hunting begins by the middle of February. In the northern states and Canada, it begins in mid- or late March. So your nesting box should be built and mounted well before then. If you have made more than one box, place them at least 100 yards apart to satisfy the bluebirds' territorial instincts.

Remember, too, that not everybody loves birds. Try to locate your box or boxes in places where they won't attract much attention.

You can attach your bluebird house to a wooden or metal pole, or to the trunk of an isolated tree that faces an open area and has no low branches. If you use an existing fence post or utility pole, be sure to get permission from its owners or one day you may find your nesting box has been removed.

The ideal height for a bluebird house is 3 to 5 feet from the ground to the bottom of the box. Although bluebirds are perfectly willing to live in a higher house, there are two reasons to mount it low. One is for protection from house sparrows, who don't like to nest so close to the ground. The other is for convenience — if the box is low, you will be able to reach it more easily when you want to observe the nest or clean

A pair of Eastern Bluebirds watching over their nest. In the nesting season, they stay close by.

out the house.

If you mount your nesting box on a post in a pasture, place it high enough so the animals can't rub it off. On a fence around a pasture, place it on the outside of the post. If you choose a busy area, such as a golf course or well-used nature preserve, mount your box out of reach — even though it means taking a small lightweight ladder with you when you monitor it.

Heat is something else to keep in

Bluebirds will nest only in open spaces. They are territorial, so space your boxes far apart.

direction you like.

Here's how to attach your house:

- On a wooden post or tree, screw or nail the box in place, using the holes you have drilled in the back board.
- On a metal pole, attach the house with bolts or wire. Choose a 6- or 7-foot length of U-post, drive it into the ground about a foot, and attach the box to the flat side. Or you may choose a ½-inch or ¾-inch galvanized pipe with threads at one end. Attach a pipe flange to the bottom of the box. Plant the unthreaded end of the pipe at least 1½ feet into the ground. Then twist the birdhouse onto the threaded end of the pipe at the top.

mind. If the temperature in your area often goes above 95 degrees Fahrenheit (35 degrees Celsius), place the house where it will be somewhat shaded during the hottest part of the day, perhaps on the north or northeast side of a large pole or on the trunk of an isolated tree. But *don't* put it in among the branches of the tree or in the woods. If you don't live in a hot part of the country, you can safely mount the nesting box in a sunny location and face it in any

If you live in an area where house sparrows are a serious problem and always take over your nesting box before bluebirds can move in, then you may want to try putting up "jug houses" made out of empty plastic bleach bottles. Though bluebirds much prefer wooden boxes, they will accept jugs if no other homes are available. On the other hand, house sparrows don't seem to like them as well. Neither do tree swallows, who are very competitive with bluebirds for homes in some parts of the Northeast.

Jug houses are much simpler to make

Feeding the nestlings is a full-time job for both parents. Babies eat about every 20 minutes.

the outside with three coats, using an exterior latex paint. Choose white or yellow or another very pale color that will reflect the heat and keep the inside of the jug cool enough for the birds.

Just like the hole in a wooden nesting box, the entrance hole in a jug house must be exactly 1½ inches in diameter (or 1$\frac{9}{16}$ inches to accommodate the larger Mountain Bluebirds), no more and no less. Since the hole must be cut with a sharp knife or a power drill with a hole saw, be extremely careful or ask an experienced adult to cut the hole for you. Directions for making a jug house are on page 30.

To attach the house to a post, you will need an 8-inch piece of wire. Curve it slightly and pass it through one of the two holes you have punched (near the bottom of the jug under the handle) and out the second hole. Hold the jug against the mounting post and wrap the wire around it, twisting the wire tightly with a pair of pliers. Insert a second piece of 8-inch wire through the hole formed by the jug's handle and wrap it around the post, securing it with the pliers as before.

Now, whether you have made a wooden nesting box or a jug house, you are ready to welcome your first guests in the spring.

than wooden boxes, and the bottles don't cost you anything. You will need the large 1-gallon size with a cap.

The jug must be well insulated with paint because it holds heat. Always cover

24

How to Make Bluebird Nesting Boxes

There are many kinds of nesting boxes that are acceptable to bluebirds if you are sure to follow the specifications (such as the size of the entrance hole) that we have discussed. The directions that follow, courtesy of the North American Bluebird Society, are for two simple boxes you can make – one opens from the top, the other from the side.

The first set of plans gives dimensions that are suitable for Eastern or Western Bluebirds. The second set includes slightly larger dimensions that are appropriate for Mountain Bluebirds. The styles of these boxes are interchangeable for bluebirds will use either one. If you prefer a side-opening box for Eastern or Western Bluebirds, or a top-opening box for Mountain Bluebirds, that's fine. Just be sure to use the dimensions that are suited to the species of bluebird you want to attract.

TOP-OPENING NESTING BOX
(Sized for Eastern and Western Bluebirds)

Materials needed:
   Lumber: ¾ inch thick, cut to the dimensions shown in the diagrams. Remember to cut off the corners of the bottom board to provide openings for ventilation and drainage.
   Dowel: ½ inch in diameter, 6½ inches long
   Cleat: ¾ inch by ⅝ inch by ⅞ inch, 3¹⁵⁄₁₆ inches long
   Screw: 1½-inch wood screw with washer
   Nails: 1¾-inch galvanized siding nails or aluminum nails
   Tools: saw, hammer, screwdriver, drill, expansion bit, and hand auger.
   Optional: paint (light color), wood sealer, or spar varnish

1. Drill the holes in the back board as shown in the diagram. These will be used to mount the box.
2. Drill three ⅛-inch holes in the dowel for easy nailing.
3. Using the expansion bit and hand auger, carefully cut the entrance hole into the front board – it cannot be even a tiny bit larger than 1½ inches in diameter. (Or ask an experienced adult to cut it with a 1½-inch hole saw attached to a power drill.)
4. Place the 10¾-inch edge of the side boards on the back board 2 inches

from the top, making sure the edges are square. Nail the back board to each side piece, spacing the nails about 3 inches apart.

5. Nail the front board to the two sides, flush to the bottom of the side boards, spacing the nails about 3 inches apart.

6. Cut the end of the top board at an angle to fit flush with the back board.

7. Holding the top board in place, nail the dowel to the back board (see finished illustration).

8. While holding the top board in place, reach through the bottom of the box and place the cleat in the correct position. Remove the top and the cleat, holding them together securely. Move the cleat about $\frac{1}{16}$ inch toward the back board and nail it in place.

9. Slide the bottom board $\frac{1}{4}$ inch up into the box (see side-view diagram). Nail it securely around all four sides.

10. With the top board in position, drill a $\frac{3}{16}$-inch hole through that board to about $\frac{1}{2}$ inch into the upper edge of the front board (see side view). This is for the wood screw.

11. Secure the top board with the screw and washer. Later, to monitor the box, you will remove this screw so you can open the top.

12. For finishing and mounting instructions, see pages 19–24.

Note: If you live in a hot climate with temperatures often above 95 degrees Fahrenheit (35 degrees Celsius), it is a good idea to drill ventilation holes at the top of the side and back boards.

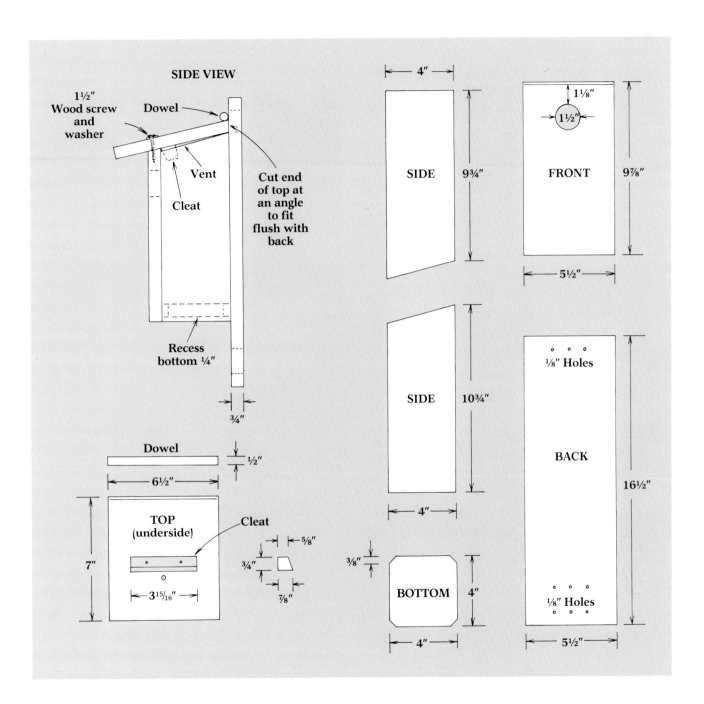

SIDE VIEW

1½"
Wood screw
and
washer

Dowel

Cut end
of top at
an angle
to fit
flush with
back

Vent

Cleat

Recess
bottom ¼"

¾"

Dowel

½"

6½"

TOP
(underside)

Cleat

7"

3¹⁵⁄₁₆"

⅝"

¾"

⅞"

4"

SIDE

9¾"

FRONT

1⅛"

1½"

9⅞"

5½"

SIDE

10¾"

4"

BACK

⅛" Holes

16½"

⅛" Holes

3⅜"

BOTTOM

4"

4"

5½"

27

SIDE-OPENING NESTING BOX
(Sized for Mountain Bluebirds)

Materials needed:

    Lumber: ¾ inch thick, cut to the dimensions shown in the diagram. Remember to cut off the corners of the bottom board to provide openings for ventilation and drainage.

    Screw: 1½-inch wood screw with washer

    Nails: 1½-inch galvanized siding nails or aluminum nails

    Tools: saw, hammer, screwdriver, drill, expansion bit, and hand auger

    Optional: mounting wire; paint (light color), wood sealer, or spar varnish

1. Drill holes in the back board as shown in the diagram. These will be used to mount the box with screws, nails, or mounting wire.
2. Using the expansion bit or hand auger, carefully cut the entrance hole into the front board – it cannot be even a tiny bit larger than 1⁹/₁₆ inches. (Or ask an experienced adult to cut it with a hole saw attached to a power drill.)
3. Place the 10½-inch edge of one of the side boards on the back board 3 inches from the bottom. Nail the back board to this side piece, spacing the nails about 3 inches apart. (The second side board will be attached later.)
4. Nail the front board to the side board, flush with the bottom of the side board, spacing the nails about 3

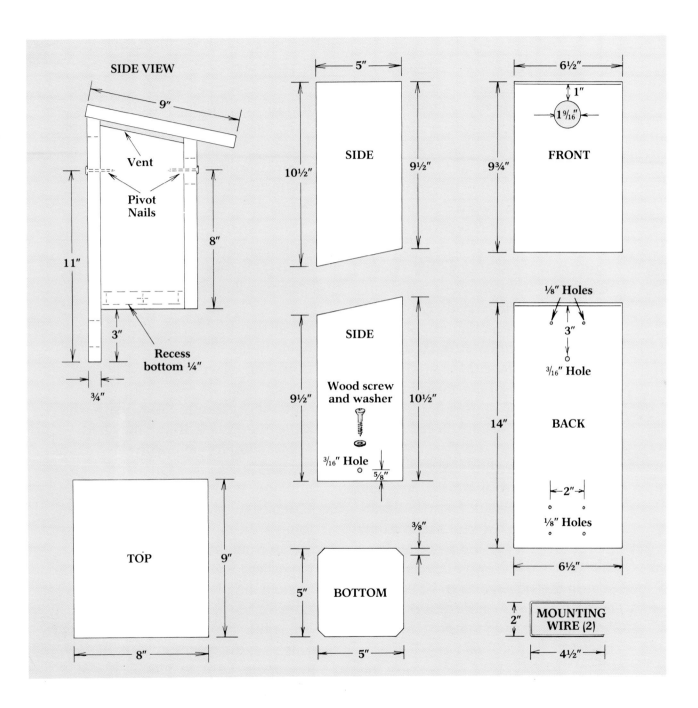

SIDE VIEW

9"

Vent

Pivot Nails

11"

8"

3"

¾"

Recess bottom ¼"

5"

SIDE

10½"

9½"

SIDE

9½"

10½"

Wood screw and washer

³⁄₁₆" Hole

⅝"

TOP

9"

8"

BOTTOM

5"

5"

⅜"

6½"

1"

1 ⁹⁄₁₆"

FRONT

9¾"

⅛" Holes

3"

³⁄₁₆" Hole

BACK

14"

2"

⅛" Holes

6½"

MOUNTING WIRE (2)

2"

4½"

inches apart.

5. Position the top board as shown in the diagram and nail to the front board and back board, again spacing the nails about 3 inches apart.

6. Insert the bottom board so that it is recessed ¼ inch from the bottom of the side and front boards, as shown in the diagram. Nail it securely to the three sides.

7. Position the remaining side board flush with the bottom of the front board, as shown in the diagram. Using a nail as a pivot point, 8 inches from the bottom of the front board, attach the front board to the side board.

8. Using another nail as a pivot point, 11 inches from the bottom of the back board, attach the back board to the side board.

9. Measuring ⅝ inch up from the bottom of the sideboard, drill a ³⁄₁₆-inch hole through this side board to about ½ inch into the edge of the bottom board. This is for the wood screw. Use the wood screw with washer to secure the side board to the bottom board (see finished illustration).

10. For finishing and mounting instructions, see pages 19–24.

JUG HOUSE

Materials needed:

Jug: 1-gallon plastic bleach bottle with cap

Paint: exterior latex in a light color

Wire: two 8-inch pieces (for attaching to post)

Tools: sharp knife or power drill with hole-saw attachment; rounded wood file or piece of sandpaper; screwdriver or large nail

1. Wash the jug thoroughly, rinsing it many times.

2. Cover the jug with three coats of light-colored paint.

3. Cut the entrance hole, using the knife or power drill. You may have to ask an adult for help with this. Make the hole precisely 1½ inches in diameter (or 1⁹⁄₁₆ inches for Mountain Bluebirds, which are larger). The bottom of the hole should be about 6 inches from the base of the jug on the opposite side from the handle.

4. Smooth the edges of the entrance hole with the file or sandpaper.

5. Using the screwdriver or nail, punch four or five drainage holes in the bottom of the jug. Also punch a hole just

Jug houses, made out of empty plastic bleach bottles, are easier to make than wooden boxes.

MONITORING THE BIRDHOUSE

After you have built and mounted your bluebird house, you will need to wait patiently for the birds to move in. If you're very lucky, they will choose your house right away. If you're not quite so lucky, they may come the next year. Getting the first pair of birds to settle in your house is the hardest part. Once they make a home there, however, your bluebird population will probably grow larger every year if you build more houses for them and put them in the right places.

Meanwhile, you have several important jobs to do. During the nesting season, you should inspect the birdhouse at least once a week. Every day is even better. You will need to remove the nest of any house sparrows who have decided you've made the house just for them. These birds are the bluebirds' greatest enemy because they not only take over the nesting sites but will kill adult birds as well as babies and eggs. You don't have to be concerned about starlings settling in if you have made the entrance hole the right size.

Don't feel sorry for the house sparrows you throw out – they won't be homeless for

below the jug handle for ventilation and two holes on the handle side about 2 inches apart and about 1 inch from the jug bottom.

6. For mounting instructions, see page 24.

long. They don't require special birdhouses or even holes for their nests. Like starlings, they will happily nest almost anywhere. Even if you evict the house sparrows after they have laid some eggs, they will just build a new nest and lay new eggs.

You will learn to recognize a house sparrow's straw and weed nest, which is usually lined with feathers and trash such as paper, plastic, and pieces of cloth. It is bulky, deep, and often domed at the top, with an entrance on the side. Sparrows' eggs are gray-white with gray or brown speckles.

Bluebirds' nests are made almost entirely of dry grasses or pine needles, and are quite neatly arranged. The best way to find out whose nest is in your birdhouse is to sit quietly a safe distance away and watch to see what kinds of birds go into it.

House sparrows are very stubborn. They may return again and again to the bluebird house, starting new nests. But you must be stubborn, too. Remove them — every day if necessary. They will eventually find somewhere else to live. Removing a nest from a nesting box is quite simple. All you have to do is reach in and take it out. For a jug house, the task is a little harder. Take a wire coat hanger and open it up into a long piece of wire hooked at one end.

Then, unscrew the jug's cap, push the wire into the jug, and pull out the nest with the hook. If you prefer, you may take the jug off its post, take it home with you, and remove the nest by hosing it out before you hang it up again.

Don't other birds use bluebird houses? Yes, they do. And many of them are just as nice to have around as bluebirds, although they may not be as beautiful. If other native hole-nesting birds, such as chickadees, titmice, tree swallows, flycatchers, or nuthatches, move into your house, don't send them packing. Let them stay, put up some more nesting boxes, and hope for bluebirds the next time around.

To keep other birds less interested in moving into your bluebird box, be careful where you mount it. Mounting a nesting box on a tree may invite house wrens as well as climbing predators such as snakes and raccoons. House wrens are also likely to take first crack at the box when it is placed too close to brushy or wooded areas, so keep it out in the open.

One problem with house wrens is that they don't always choose an empty box for themselves. Sometimes they throw a bluebird family's eggs or nestlings out of the nest and take over the box, building their own twig nest right on top of the old one.

A young bluebird who is almost ready to leave the nest takes a quick peek at the outside world.

These little bluebirds, only 12 days old, are always ready for a snack of insects or berries.

Another problem is that male house wrens often claim a few nesting boxes, stuffing each of them with a lot of little sticks. Then the female comes along and chooses one she wants as a nest site. If one of your boxes is filled to the brim, not with a nest, but only with sticks, feel free to remove them to make room for a bluebird family.

To discourage house sparrows, avoid areas that are heavily populated by them, such as farms and urban areas. And remember to toss them out immediately if they move into your box.

Your last job of the year is an easy one, but it is very important, too. In the fall or winter, give your nesting box a final inspection. Take out any old nests, wash the box if a hose is handy, make any necessary repairs, and be sure the drainage holes are open. Go back again in the very early spring and check the box once more. This time, you may find mice using it for a cozy home. If you do, evict them—they will find new quarters for themselves.

Your birdhouse is now ready for occupancy when the bluebirds return again.

Bluebirds may die from starvation if their winter supply of berries gets covered with snow and ice.

BLUEBIRD CARE AND FEEDING

In the winter and early spring, when insects are scarce and bluebirds turn to berries, you may be able to lure the birds to your nesting box with food if they remain in your part of the country all year. (They will enjoy a bird bath, too.) Most berries, such as strawberries and blueberries, don't last until winter. But there are some that get hard and tough and do not drop off no matter how strong the wind blows or how low the temperature drops. Although these berries may not look very good to us, the birds are happy to eat them when they are hungry.

Some berry plants, like sumac, are wild. Others must be purchased at a nursery. Be sure that you find out how to plant them correctly.

Listed below are some of the most common plants whose berries appeal to bluebirds and many other desirable birds. Some of them have berries that last well into the winter. Of course, not every berry tree, shrub, or vine will grow everywhere, so it is important to find out which ones will survive in your climate:

American holly | Mistletoe
Bayberry | Mountain ash
(wax myrtle) | Mulberry
Bittersweet | Multiflora rose
Black alder | Pin cherry
Black cherry | Pyracantha
Common | (firethorn)
chokeberry | Red cedar
Dogwood | Shadberry
Elderberry | (serviceberry)
Hackberry | Sumac
Hawthorn | Virginia creeper
Honeysuckle | Wild grape

Bluebirds prefer to eat insects but, in the winter, their main source of food is hard berries.

Though bluebirds don't eat seeds and so aren't interested in the usual kinds of outdoor bird food, you can fill a feeder with other food they *do* like: raisins and other dried fruits, chopped unsalted nuts, suet, finely cracked corn or cornmeal, or peanut hearts. If there are bluebirds in your neighborhood in the winter or early spring, you may find them eating at your feeder.

When bluebirds are living in your birdhouse, try not to bother them too much. You can easily frighten them away, especially while they are building their nest. Until the nest is completed and the eggs are laid, observe only from a distance. After that, they won't mind too much if you open the box and take a very fast look once in a while just to see what is going on. Then close the box again very quickly. To check on the occupants of a jug house, just look into the entrance hole.

Never, never touch the nest or the eggs or the baby birds. (Exception: If there are dead birds, remove them with a paper towel or a pair of tongs and bury them. And of course, it's always a good idea to wash your hands afterward.) Before you open the box, tap the side lightly to warn the mother you are there and give her a chance to fly away. Don't disturb the box after the nestlings are about two weeks old and getting themselves geared up to leave home in another week or so. If you bother them now, they may leave too early to survive.

Cats, raccoons, opossums, snakes, squirrels, weasels, and skunks all consider birds or eggs to be tasty snacks. They will climb up poles and trees and reach inside nests for food. You have already helped protect your bluebird family from its enemies by making your nesting box the right depth with the entrance hole in the right place. But if there are many climbing animals in your area, you can protect the birds in other ways. You can, for example, mount the house on a thin metal pole and then keep the pole very slippery. Spread soft automobile grease on the pole every week or so during the nesting season. The grease must be fresh, because if it hardens, it may make the pole even easier for an animal to climb.

You can also make a "raccoon guard" to attach to the entrance hole of the nesting box. Take a board 1½ to 2 inches thick and about 3 inches square. Cut a hole in it exactly 1½ inches (or 1⁹/₁₆ inches) in diameter to match the entrance hole. Nail or screw it to the front of the box, lining up the two holes. This thick board will make it much harder for an animal – or a starling – to reach inside far enough to get to the nest.

A different way to discourage predators is to attach a metal shield around the post below the birdhouse. This can be a wide, flat metal collar, or, even better, a metal baffle that has been shaped into a cone. Point the wide end down. Mount the guard just below the box, nailing or wiring it in place high enough so an animal cannot jump over it from the ground. If you prefer, you can make a guard out of an upside-down plastic wastebasket, cutting a hole in the bottom small enough so the basket will cling to the pole just below the nesting box. Cut off any rim so animals can't use it as a foothold. Put the guard on the pole before you plant the pole in the ground.

And here's yet another good method of fending off creeping and leaping predators: buy a flat 24-inch square piece of hardware cloth (¼-inch wire mesh), cut a hole in the very center to closely fit around the pole, and slide it onto the pole directly below the nesting box. Hold it in place with a piece of wire that loops over the top of the box. Again, put this guard on before planting the pole in the ground.

There's not very much you can do to protect bluebirds from the cold, another enemy, except to leave your nesting box in place all year. Sometimes birds will huddle together in it during bad weather, especially at night. In some areas where bluebirds stay all year, people make special winter roosting boxes with enough room for quite a few chilly birds.

Sometimes people are a bird's worst enemy. Whether they are mean or just curious, people may disturb the birds so much they will fly away and never come back. Sometimes they even destroy the nests or knock down the boxes. That's why it's so important to mount your house in an out-of-the-way place and, if necessary, above eye level. Talk to your friends, neighbors, and family about your bluebird project. Explain that the birdhouse must not be disturbed.

If vandalism by people is a problem in your area, perhaps a small waterproof notice attached in an obvious place on the front or side of your box will help protect the bluebirds. It might be as simple as: "This is a bluebird nesting box, part of an international effort to increase the population of bluebirds. Please do not touch." Or, "Built for a bluebird family. Please do not touch."

If you wish, you could add: "For more information, contact a local birding organization or the North American Bluebird Society, P.O. Box 6295, Silver Spring, MD 20916-6295." Some people even include their own names and telephone numbers so they can answer questions about bluebird conservation.

Once the young bluebirds leave the nest, they won't return, living instead in trees and bushes. To encourage their parents to raise another brood the same year, take out the old nest as soon as possible, unless they have already begun to build another nest on top of the old one. In that case, leave it alone. You may not have to wait long this time for new bluebird neighbors.

BUILDING A BLUEBIRD TRAIL

If you and your friends get together, you can start a bluebird trail – the best way to attract a large number of the birds to your neighborhood. A bluebird trail is simply many bluebird houses mounted one after another in a continuous line. The houses must be at least 100 yards apart. The line may be quite straight, perhaps along the sides of a country road. Or it may be curved or circular, maybe going around a farm, a golf course, or even a whole village. It can be short, with only a dozen birdhouses or so. Or it can be very long, going on for miles and miles, with hundreds of houses.

Many bluebird trails are organized and maintained by young people, often working with Scout or Camp Fire groups or with 4-H, garden, and bird clubs. Sometimes bluebird trails are classroom projects, with students learning about bluebirds while helping them to survive.

The reason for lining up nesting boxes in a trail is to make monitoring easier. The circular trail that starts and ends at the same place is the easiest of all. During nesting season, you can make your

This Eastern male has found a natural hole where his mate is building a nest for the family.

weekly inspection on foot, on a bicycle or a horse, or riding in a car, moving along from one nesting box to the next.

If you would like to make your own trail, here are some important tips to keep in mind:

Start out small. Don't build more houses than you will be able to monitor. You can always add others or start new trails later on.

Remember to locate the houses at least 100 yards apart because these territorial birds insist on their space.

Number the houses so you can easily keep records of the eggs laid and the babies hatched.

Attach a small weatherproof label to each birdhouse, telling your name or the name of your group along with a message like "Please do not disturb. Help save the bluebirds."

Divide the responsibility for sections of the trail among different people or groups if your trail becomes very long.

Recruit a leader. Your group leader, a parent, or a responsible young person may agree to be in charge.

Don't forget to make your trail in the right environment (open space, scattered trees, short vegetation, an area not too close to many buildings and people) and with the houses properly spaced, or all your work may be wasted. And, of course, if your trail will cross public or private property, you must get permission for it before you begin.

Remember that it may take time for the bluebirds to find your houses and decide to settle down there. In the meantime, be sure some members of your group monitor the boxes from early spring through August so they will always be clean and free of uninvited guests. All your work will be rewarded when bluebirds come home to live in your neighborhood again after an absence of so many years.

Whenever you see these beautiful little birds flashing through the skies or perching peacefully on the homes you have made for them, remember that you have helped to rescue them. You are among the thousands of people across the continent who have written a story with a happy ending for America's favorite bird, the "bluebird of happiness."

GLOSSARY

brood (noun)
birds hatched and raised together.

brood (verb)
to sit over the eggs to keep them warm.

clutch
a cluster or group.

extinct
no longer existing.

fledgling
a young bird that has just acquired the feathers it needs to fly.

habitat
the place where an animal naturally lives or a plant naturally grows.

incubate
to keep eggs at a certain temperature so they will hatch; birds incubate their eggs by sitting over them.

instinct
behavior that occurs naturally, that does not have to be learned.

migrate
to move periodically from one area to another for food and breeding.

molt
to shed feathers.

nestling
a young bird that has not yet left the nest.

predator
an animal that preys upon another.

species
a group of plants or animals that are similar to one another and reproduce almost solely among themselves; there are three species of bluebirds: Eastern, Western, and Mountain.

thrush
the family of birds to which all three species of bluebirds belong.

toxic
harmful, poisonous.

vandalism
malicious destruction.

RESOURCE LIST

VIDEOS

Bluebirds Up Close by Michael Godfrey, Nature Science Network. Bird Watcher's Digest, Box 110, Marietta, OH 45750; 800-879-2473.

Jewels of Blue: The Story of the Eastern Bluebird by Boz Metzdorf. Bird's Eye View Productions, 3060 S. St. Croix Trail, Afton, MN 55001; 612-436-5972.

Bluebird Trails: How to Start and Maintain a Bluebird Trail by Boz Metzdorf. Bird's Eye View Productions, 3060 S. St. Croix Trail, Afton, MN 55001; 612-436-5972.

Backyard Blues: Observing Bluebirds in Your Backyard by Boz Metzdorf. Bird's Eye View Productions, 3060 S. St. Croix Trail, Afton, MN 55001; 612-436-5972.

Bluebirds — Bring Them Back by Walter Berlet. Berlet Films, 1646 West Kimmel Road, Jackson, MI 49201; 517-784-6969.*

Audubon Society's Visual Guide to the Birds of North America, Volume 4. Mastervision, 969 Park Avenue, New York, NY 10028; 212-879-0448.

SLIDE PROGRAM

Where Have All the Bluebirds Gone? by the North American Bluebird Society. North American Bluebird Society, P.O. Box 6295, Silver Spring, MD 20916-6295; 301-384-2798. For rent or purchase.*

BOOKS

The Bluebird: How You Can Help Its Fight for Survival by Lawrence Zeleny. Indiana University Press.*

The Bluebird Book by Donald and Lillian Stokes. Little, Brown.*

A Guide to Bird Behavior by Donald and Lillian Stokes. Volume 3. Little, Brown.*

The Complete Birdhouse Book by Donald and Lillian Stokes. Little, Brown.*

Bluebirds in the Upper Midwest: A Guide to Successful Trail Management by Dorene Scriven. Audubon Recovery Chapter of Minneapolis, Box 3801, Minneapolis, MN 55403; 612-922-4586.

Bluebird chorus: Five nestlings wait for their meal. Soon they'll be big enough to leave home.

Bluebirds: Their Daily Lives and How to Attract and Raise Bluebirds by Tina Dew et al. Nature Book Publishers, P.O. Box 115, Valley Lee, MD 20692; 301-994-1662.*

Mountain Bluebird Management by Brian R. Shantz. Ellis Bird Farm, P.O. Box 2980, Lacombe, Alberta, Canada T0C 1S0; 403-346-211.

Beakless Bluebirds and Featherless Penguins by Sister Barbara Ann. Scriptorium Publications, P.O. Box 3127, Catonsville, MD 21228-0127; 301-747-4104.*

Bluebirds! by Steve Grooms and Dick Peterson. NorthWord Press, P.O. Box 1360, Minocqua, WI 54548; 800-336-5666.

The Mountain Bluebird by Ron Hirschi. E.P. Dutton, Cobblehill Books (juvenile).

NEWSLETTERS AND JOURNALS

Sialia, the Quarterly Journal of the North American Bluebird Society. NABS, Box 6295, Silver Spring, MD 20916-6295; 301-384-2798. Subscription price is included in annual membership dues ($15; $10 student or senior).

Nature Society News, a monthly newspaper about purple martins, bluebirds, and other birds. The Nature Society, Griggsville, IL 62340; 217-833-2323. Membership includes newspaper: $12 per year.

Bird Watcher's Digest, a bi-monthly magazine. Bird Watcher's Digest, Box 110, Marietta, OH 45750; 800-879-2473. Subscription: $15.95 per year.

Bluebird News, a monthly newsletter. Bluebird News, P.O. Box 1624, Mount Pleasant, TX 75456; 903-572-7529. Subscription: $20 per year (over 65, $15).

*Note: All items marked with an asterisk (*) are available from the North American Bluebird Society, P.O. Box 6295, Silver Spring, MD 20916-6295, in addition to the listed sources.

INDEX

ILLUSTRATION AND PHOTOGRAPHY CREDITS

Christopher Clapp, p. 26-29

Isidor Jeklin, p. 5, 19, 40

Maslowski Wildlife Productions, p. 6, 7, 9, 10, 11, 12, 14, 17, 18, 21, 33 (left), 34, 35, 36

David Middleton, p. 13 (left)

Lorne Scott, p. 13 (right)

Michael L. Smith, p. 4, 15, 16, 22, 23, 31, 33 (right), 39, 44

Edward Kanze, p. 24

ABOUT THE AUTHOR

Joan Rattner Heilman is a longstanding bluebird enthusiast. When her children were young, she recalls offering them a reward for spotting her favorite bird. They never did and neither did she — an experience they all remember as a dramatic illustration of the bluebird's plight. Ms. Heilman is a freelance writer and author of many books, for adults as well as children. She and her husband, an engineer, have three grown children and reside in Mamaroneck, New York.